Mini-Meditations
for Lent

Daniel L. Lowery, C.Ss.R.

Liguori
ONE LIGUORI DRIVE
LIGUORI MO 63057-9999

Imprimi Potest:
John F. Dowd, C.Ss.R.
Provincial, St. Louis Province
The Redemptorists

Imprimatur:
+ Edward J. O'Donnell
Vicar General, Archdiocese of St. Louis

ISBN 978-0-7648-1769-4
Copyright © 1985, Liguori Publications
Printed in the United States of America
08 09 10 11 4 3 2 1

Scripture texts used in this work are taken from the *New American
Bible,* copyright © 1970, by the Confraternity of Christian Doctrine,
Washington, D.C., and are used by permission of copyright owner.
All rights reserved.

Liguori Publications, a nonprofit corporation, is an apostolate
of the Redemptorists. To learn more about the Redemptorists,
visit Redemptorists.com.

To order, call 800-325-9521
www.liguori.org

Mini-Meditations
for Lent

Daniel L. Lowery, C.Ss.R.

Prayerful meditation for a few minutes each day on one of the main themes of Lent can make all the difference between vaguely acknowledging Lent as special and actually making it so.

Try reading the few verses here offered from each day's Mass—*slowly.* Then pause for some minutes (as many as you can spare!) to let those words of the Lord speak to you. Finally, respond to the Lord in simple prayer.

Each Scripture reading presented

here may easily be expanded by locating the verse in its context and reading the entire section. The brief, prayerful reflection may serve as a springboard for your own personal prayer.

Ash Wednesday

Rend your hearts, not your garments, and return to the LORD, your God (Joel 2:13).

Lord, during these days of Lent, I want to open my mind and heart to you so that I can be intimately touched by your grace.

Thursday after Ash Wednesday

Whoever wishes to be my follower must deny his very self, take up his cross each day, and follow in my steps (Luke 9:23).

Lord, help me not to be afraid of self-denial and the cross; give me the grace to follow you today.

Friday after Ash Wednesday

*Do you call this a fast,
a day acceptable to the
LORD? (Isaiah 58:5)*

Lord, I want to fast and abstain during Lent, but I also want to heed the warning of your prophet Isaiah, that my fast and abstinence be not an end in themselves but a spur to greater love and justice in my life.

Saturday after Ash Wednesday

I have not come to invite the self-righteous to a change of heart, but sinners (Luke 5:32).

Lord, I freely acknowledge that I am a sinner and in need of a change of heart; help me to accept your invitation today.

Sunday, First Week of Lent

Then Jesus was led into the desert by the Spirit to be tempted by the devil (Matthew 4:1).

Lord, I am aware of many temptations in my life, but today I draw new courage from your example of fidelity in rejecting the devil and all his works and all his empty promises.

Monday, First Week of Lent

Be holy, for I, the LORD, your God, am holy (Leviticus 19:2).

Though I do not always act like it, Lord, I really do want to be holy; I ask your grace to imitate your holiness in my life.

Tuesday, First Week of Lent

This is how you are to pray:
Our Father in heaven
(Matthew 6:9).

Thank you, Lord, for teaching us the way to pray; as I now slowly pray the prayer you taught us, let the truth of it strike deep roots in my heart.

Wednesday, First Week of Lent

At the judgment, the citizens of Nineveh will rise along with the present generation, and they will condemn it (Luke 11:32).

Lord, the citizens of Nineveh, unlike "the present generation," had the humility and wisdom to repent; grant me, during this Lent, the same humility and wisdom.

Thursday, First Week of Lent

Ask, and you will receive. Seek, and you will find. Knock, and it will be opened to you (Matthew 7:7).

Your promises, Lord, are music to my ears; I desire today to have absolute confidence that you will hear and answer my prayers.

Friday, First Week of Lent

If you bring your gift to the altar and there recall that your brother has anything against you, leave your gift at the altar, go first to be reconciled with your brother, and then come and offer your gift Matthew 5:23-24).

Because of my pride and stubbornness, Lord, I find it hard to be reconciled to some of my brothers and sisters; today I beg you for the grace to work for reconciliation with others and to be open to reconciliation when your grace is at work through others.

Saturday, First Week of Lent

My command to you is: love your enemies, pray for your persecutors (Matthew 5:44).

Once again I pray, Lord, to be freed from the chains of hatred, resentment, and revenge that choke me; create within me a new heart and a new spirit.

Sunday, Second Week of Lent

He was transfigured before their eyes (Matthew 17:2).

Your Transfiguration, Lord, is a beautiful reminder to me, as it was to your first disciples, that your power and glory will ultimately overcome the darkness of evil in the world; help me to be renewed in the spirit of hope today.

Monday, Second Week of Lent

Be compassionate, as your Father is compassionate (Luke 6:36).

I often lack compassion toward others, Lord, even though I long for it myself; give me a new heart, full of compassion toward my brothers and sisters.

Tuesday, Second Week of Lent

Whoever exalts himself shall be humbled, but whoever humbles himself shall be exalted (Matthew 23:12).

Most of the "conventional wisdom" I hear every day tells me that humility is for losers, Lord; but today let me listen to your wisdom which tells me that humility is really for winners.

Wednesday, Second Week of Lent

Anyone among you who aspires to greatness must serve the rest, and whoever wants to rank first among you must serve the needs of all (Matthew 20:26-27).

I aspire to the greatness of being one of your disciples, Lord; I have many opportunities—at home, at work, in my neighborhood, in my parish—to serve; give me the grace to do it.

Thursday, Second Week of Lent

Once there was a rich man who dressed in purple and linen and feasted splendidly every day (Luke 16:19).

Sometimes I get my priorities mixed up, Lord, and I begin to think that clothing and food and material possessions are much more important than they really are; let this Lent be a time of rearranging my priorities in light of your Gospel.

Friday, Second Week of Lent

With that they seized him, dragged him outside the vineyard, and killed him (Matthew 21:39).

I recall this parable, Lord, and I know that it speaks to me of your suffering and death; I know that your sufferings and death have set me free, and I am deeply grateful.

Saturday, Second Week of Lent

You will cast into the depths of the sea all our sins (Micah 7:19).

I carry with me, Lord, the burden of sin and guilt; but today I am joyful in the realization that you are loving enough to forgive my sins and take away my guilt.

Sunday, Third Week of Lent

Everyone who drinks this water
will be thirsty again.
But whoever drinks the water
   I will give him will never be
thirsty (John 4:13-14).

My spirit is often dry and thirsty, Lord; I pray today that I may avidly receive the living water of your word and your Spirit.

Monday, Third Week of Lent

But his [Nathan's] servants...
said, "if the prophet had told you
to do something extraordinary,
would you not have done it?"
(2 Kings 5:13)

This story of Nathan is a good reminder for me, Lord. He was looking for some extraordinary healing event and almost rejected the ordinary means offered to him. I do that a lot, and so I ask you to help me see your will in the ordinary things of my life.

Tuesday, Third Week of Lent

Then Peter came up and asked him, "Lord, when my brother wrongs me, how often must I forgive him?" (Matthew 18:21)

Your answer to Peter, Lord, "seventy times seven times," means that our forgiveness, like yours, must be without limit; help me today to forgive from my heart all who have hurt me in any way.

Wednesday, Third Week of Lent

For what great nation is there that has gods so close to it as the LORD, our God, is to us whenever we call upon him? (Deuteronomy 4:7)

I so easily forget, Lord, how near you are to me; give me the grace to be more aware of your life-giving presence at every moment of my life.

Thursday, Third Week of Lent

They walked in the hardness of their evil hearts and turned their backs, not their faces, to me (Jeremiah 7:24).

Your prophet Jeremiah gives a profound description of sin, Lord; I have often turned my back, not my face, to you; I repent today of all my sins.

Friday, Third Week of Lent

*One of the scribes came up, and…
decided to ask him, "Which is the
first of all the commandments?"
(Mark 12:28)*

I know how you answered the scribe,
Lord, and emphasized that the first of
the commandments is love; I stand in
need of the grace to love you with all
my heart, soul, mind, and strength.

Saturday, Third Week of Lent

He [Jesus] then spoke this parable addressed to those who believed in their own self-righteousness while holding everyone else in contempt (Luke 18:9).

Your parable about the proud Pharisee and the humble tax collector, Lord, is one that I need to remember; I am often self-righteous and hold others in contempt; once again I pray for a change of heart.

Sunday, Fourth Week of Lent

I know this much: I was blind before; now I can see (John 9:25).

I am spiritually blind, Lord, but you are the light of the world; light up the blind spots of my heart.

Monday, Fourth Week of Lent

The man put his trust in the word Jesus spoke to him, and started for home (John 4:50).

Unlike the royal official referred to here, Lord, I am often afraid to trust in your word; help me today to learn to "let go and let God."

Tuesday, Fourth Week of Lent

Remember, now, you have been cured. Give up your sins so that something worse may not overtake you (John 5:14).

I have been cured in the life-giving waters of Baptism, Lord; give me the grace to be faithful to my baptismal promises.

Wednesday, Fourth Week of Lent

I am not seeking my own will but the will of him who sent me (John 5:30).

My trouble is that I often seek my own will instead of yours, Lord; I pray today for the grace to seek your will in everything.

Thursday, Fourth Week of Lent

How can people like you believe,
when you accept praise from
* one another yet do not seek the*
glory that comes from
* the One [God]? (John 5:44).*

Those who rejected you, Lord, refused
to listen to you or to those who were
your witnesses; open my mind and
heart to your word.

Friday, Fourth Week of Lent

So you know me,
and you know my origins?
The truth is, I have not come of
myself. I was sent by One who
* has the right to send,*
and him you do not know
(John 7:28).

Sometimes I, like the people you were addressing, am very smug about my knowledge of you, Lord; open my mind and heart to the full mystery of who you are.

Saturday, Fourth Week of Lent

When the temple guards came back, the chief priests and Pharisees asked them, "Why did you not bring him in?" "No man ever spoke like that before," the guards replied (John 7:45-46).

The simple and unsophisticated temple guards recognized your wisdom, Lord; the chief priests did not. Give me a wise and understanding heart as I listen to your word this Lent.

Sunday, Fifth Week of Lent

I am the resurrection and the life: whoever believes in me, though he should die, will come to life; and whoever is alive and believes in me will never die (John 11:25-26).

Thank you, Lord, for this exquisite promise of eternal life with you, where "there shall be no more death or mourning, crying out or pain."

Monday, Fifth Week of Lent

The whole assembly cried aloud, blessing God who saves those that hope in him (Daniel 13:60).

I, too, bless you, Lord, and renew my hope in you, for you are my Savior and my God.

Tuesday, Fifth Week of Lent

But with their patience worn out by the journey, the people complained against God and Moses (Numbers 21:4-5).

In the desert of my life, Lord, I often complain of your will and your plan; help me today to be rid of self-pity and complaint.

Wednesday, Fifth Week of Lent

I give you my assurance, everyone who lives in sin is the slave of sin (John 8:34).

I know the truth of your words, Lord, from bitter experience; the slavery of sin takes away my freedom and integrity; liberate me today from that slavery.

Thursday, Fifth Week of Lent

I will maintain my covenant with you and your descendants after you throughout the ages as an everlasting pact, to be your God and the God of your descendants after you (Genesis 17:7).

I can never sufficiently express my gratitude to you, Lord, for your unconditional love and fidelity to us, your people; help me to be faithful in return.

Friday, Fifth Week of Lent

If I do not perform my Father's works, put no faith in me.

But if I do perform them,
even though you put no faith
in me, put faith in these works
(John 10:37-38).

Your marvelous works, Lord, both in times past and still today, speak for themselves; I put my faith in you.

Saturday, Fifth Week of Lent

He withdrew instead to a town called Ephraim in the region near the desert, where he stayed with his disciples (John 11:54).

Before facing death, Lord, you went once again to the desert to engage in prayer; help me to learn the value of prayer and solitude in the difficult times of my life.

Passion (Palm) Sunday

*Your attitude must be that of
Christ:…he emptied himself
and took the form of a slave,
being born in the likeness of
men (Philippians 2:5,7).*

As we begin this week, Lord, help me
to have a fuller and deeper appreciation
of your self-emptying love.

Monday of Holy Week

*Here is my servant whom I uphold,
my chosen one with whom
I am pleased (Isaiah 42:1).*

You have indeed been our servant,
Lord, bearing our infirmities and
enduring our sufferings; I praise you
today as Savior and Redeemer.

Tuesday of Holy Week

"Lord," Peter said to him, "why can I not follow you now? I will lay down my life for you!" (John 13:37).

Peter, the Rock on which you built your Church, Lord, was brave until the going got rough, then he was weak; I can certainly relate to Peter's weakness, and so today I pray for courage and fortitude in my Christian life.

Wednesday of Holy Week

They paid him thirty pieces of silver, and from that time on he kept looking for an opportunity to hand him over (Matthew 26:15-16).

I find myself, Lord, feeling immensely sorry for Judas; somehow he didn't realize how much you loved him; give me the grace to appreciate your love more and more.

Holy Thursday

What I just did was to give you
  an example:
as I have done, so you must do
(John 13:15).

Your moving example of washing the feet of your apostles, Lord, is a strong encouragement to me; teach me how to love as you did.

Good Friday

Then he bowed his head, and delivered over his spirit (John 19:30).

Your saving death, Lord, is an overwhelming sign of the Father's love for us; let me never forget his love or yours.

Holy Saturday

If we have died with Christ, we believe that we are also to live with him (Romans 6:8).

During this Lent, Lord, I have tried to die at least a little to the sin and selfishness in me; help me really to live the new life you have given me.